Behind The Wheel™

Ryan Newman

NASCAR Driver

Simone Payment

rosen publishing's
rosen central®

New York

Published in 2007 by The Rosen Publishing Group, Inc.
29 East 21st Street, New York, NY 10010

Copyright © 2007 by The Rosen Publishing Group, Inc.

First Edition

Library of Congress Cataloging-in-Publication Data

Payment, Simone.
Ryan Newman: NASCAR driver / Simone Payment.—1st ed.
     p. cm.—(Behind the wheel)
Includes bibliographical references and index.
ISBN-13: 978-1-4042-0983-1
ISBN-10: 1-4042-0983-2 (library binding)
1. Newman, Ryan, 1977– —Juvenile literature.
2. Automobile racing drivers—United States—Biography—Juvenile literature. I. Title.
GV1032.N44P39 2007
796.72092—dc22

                                              2006021397

Manufactured in the United States of America

On the cover: Ryan Newman gets ready for the Coca-Cola 600 in May 2003 at the Lowe's Motor Speedway in North Carolina.

CONTENTS

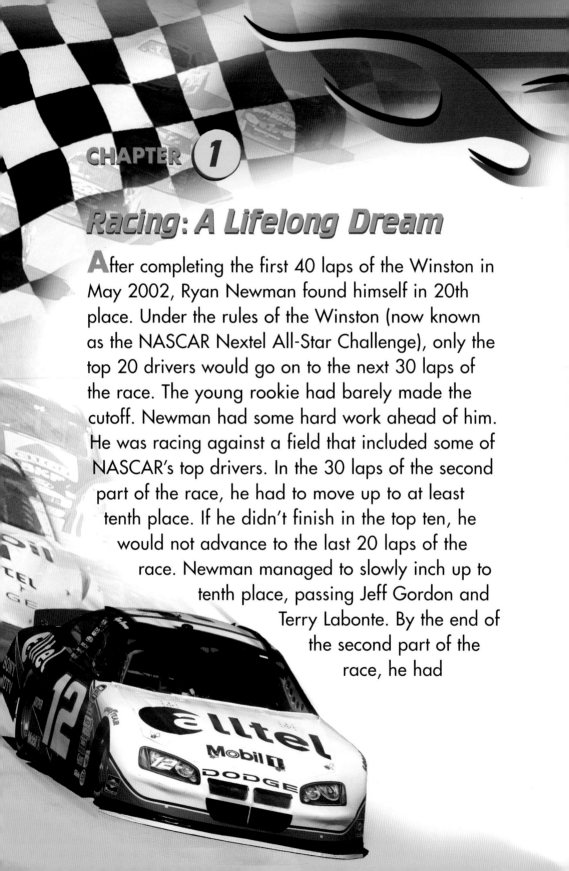

CHAPTER 1

Racing: *A Lifelong Dream*

After completing the first 40 laps of the Winston in May 2002, Ryan Newman found himself in 20th place. Under the rules of the Winston (now known as the NASCAR Nextel All-Star Challenge), only the top 20 drivers would go on to the next 30 laps of the race. The young rookie had barely made the cutoff. Newman had some hard work ahead of him. He was racing against a field that included some of NASCAR's top drivers. In the 30 laps of the second part of the race, he had to move up to at least tenth place. If he didn't finish in the top ten, he would not advance to the last 20 laps of the race. Newman managed to slowly inch up to tenth place, passing Jeff Gordon and Terry Labonte. By the end of the second part of the race, he had

Ryan Newman is pictured here after his win at the Winston, a NASCAR event similar to Major League Baseball's All-Star Game. Top drivers compete at Lowe's Motor Speedway in North Carolina.

moved up to seventh place. Newman would advance to the final 20 laps.

Twenty laps don't leave a lot of time to move up from seventh to first, but Newman was determined. Winning the race wouldn't get him any points toward winning the Winston Cup (now known as the Nextel

Cup). However, it would be a huge accomplishment for
a driver in his first full year of competing in the NASCAR
Cup series. In fact, it was an achievement for Newman
to even be in the Winston. To qualify for the race, a
driver must have won a NASCAR Cup race in the past
two years. Drivers who have won the Winston in the
past also qualify. The other way to get into the race is by

Newman is only the second driver to win the Winston after qualifying with a win in the Winston Open/No Bull 5. Most Winston winners are qualified by winning other NASCAR races.

winning a qualifying race (the Winston Open/No Bull 5 Spring), which Newman had done.

In seventh place after 70 laps, Newman had a hard road ahead of him. Luckily, he got some help from NASCAR fans. One feature of the Winston Cup is that fans vote online to determine how the racers will start for the last 20 laps of the race. In the 2002 race, fans voted to reverse the field's starting position. Instead of the first-place driver starting in the first position, he would start tenth. Newman's seventh-place standing allowed him to start in fourth place. Passing the three drivers ahead of him turned out to be easy. Holding everyone off to win the race was another story. Late in the race, Dale Earnhardt Jr. began inching closer to Newman. By the last lap, Earnhardt Jr. was directly behind Newman, his front bumper close enough to touch Newman's back bumper. With just a little push, Earnhardt Jr. could have spun Newman. This would likely have wrecked Newman's car, ending his chances for victory. Instead, Newman managed to pull away, narrowly winning the race.

Afterward, Newman was incredibly excited. He was just the second rookie to win the Winston. (Dale Earnhardt Jr. had been the first.) Even after winning other Cup races and many other awards, Newman still considers winning the Winston in 2002 to be his greatest accomplishment.

A Race Car Driver Is Born

Ryan Joseph Newman's journey to NASCAR racing began in South Bend, Indiana, on December 8, 1977. Ryan's father, Greg Newman, immediately began planning his newborn son's racing career. Ryan's grandfather was a race official at the South Bend Motor Speedway. Greg himself had done some racing when he was young, but he got into a serious accident when he was nine years old. After that, his mother wouldn't let him race.

Even though he gave up driving, Greg continued to love cars and racing. He even took his future wife, Diane, on dates to races. When Greg and Diane got married in 1975, they went to Daytona to see races on their honeymoon. Back in Indiana, Greg ran an auto-repair business. Diane helped out with the business and stayed home with Ryan and his younger sister, Jamie.

It wasn't long before Ryan caught the racing bug from his father and grandfather. By the time he was four years old, he was driving his first car on a small track in New Carlisle, Indiana. From the start, it was clear that he was a very good driver. He was so good that by the time Ryan was five, he started driving quarter midget cars in races. (Quarter midget cars are kid-sized, open-wheel race cars.)

Weekends at the Track

Quarter midget racing is for kids age five to sixteen. Races take place at dirt, concrete, or asphalt tracks. Almost every weekend during the racing season—from April to October—the Newmans would travel to a different racetrack so Ryan could compete. They would pack up their truck with a camper on the back and head to tracks as far away as Arizona and Connecticut.

Even in his first year in quarter midget racing, Ryan was winning races. When he was eight years old, he won the Junior Stock Division Quarter Midget Nationals in Lincoln, Indiana. By the time he was 11, he was winning race after race. That year, he won 17 out of 27 races he entered. He also won the Grand National Quarter Midget Championship.

Everyone in the family enjoyed racing weekends. It was a family effort, with Greg doing all the mechanical work on Ryan's cars. Eventually, Jamie started racing, too. She also helped out at the track by videotaping Ryan's races and keeping records, as well as helping with the car. Jamie and Ryan were very close and supportive of each other.

Balancing Racing with School

It was very important to Greg and Diane that their children get a good education. They decided to make some rules about racing weekends. First, the family had to be back on Monday morning in time for school. Second, Ryan and Jamie had to keep up with their chores and homework before they could leave for a racing weekend.

Even though he was very focused on racing, Ryan did well in school and excelled at math. Ryan also became a

Newman got his start racing quarter midget and midget race cars similar to the one pictured here.

very skilled mechanic. By the time he was eight, he was able to take both of his quarter midget cars apart and put them back together. During the week, he would help his father get the cars ready for that week's race. His nickname—Racin' Ryan—was painted on both of them. He used #43 as his number, in honor of his driving hero, Richard Petty. Ryan and his dad were very close, and Ryan enjoyed the time they spent together in the garage.

Even though Ryan had been driving since he was four, he didn't get his first "street" car until he was able to drive legally. On his 16th birthday, his dad gave him a 1974 Triumph TR-6 that had belonged to Ryan's grandfather. Ryan and his dad rebuilt the engine, painted the car, and soon it was ready for the road. Ryan still has this car today.

There are several famous racing families, and the Pettys are one of them. In 1959, Lee Petty became the first winner of the Daytona 500. He would go on to set a record by winning a career total of 54 races. This record stood until his son, Richard, came along. Richard (shown below) broke his father's record in 1967. That year, he won 27 out of 48 NASCAR races. On July 4, 1984, he won his 200th race. This record of 200 NASCAR wins may not ever be broken. Richard's son, Kyle, is currently a NASCAR driver. Kyle's son, Adam, was also a NASCAR driver, but he tragically died in an accident on a racetrack in Loudon, New Hampshire, in 2000.

Ryan enjoyed fishing with his grandfather on the rare summer weekends when they didn't have a race. But he didn't spend a lot of time relaxing. Most of the time, he was focused on the next race. Ryan was very competitive— even while racing slot cars with his friends. His dream, from a very early age, was to win the Daytona 500. Starting in 1990, Ryan and his dad went to the Daytona 500 every year.

The Next Step in Racing

Ryan was extremely successful in his quarter midget racing career, winning more than 100 races. In fact, he has been inducted into the Quarter Midget Hall of Fame. In 1993, when Ryan was 15, he took the next step. He began racing in the Midget Series.

In the Midget Series, people race cars similar to the ones used in quarter midget but about four times larger. However, the Midget Series is open to drivers 15 and older. The fact that Ryan was now racing against adults didn't get in the way of his winning. In his very first year, he won the season championship of the All-American Midget Series. He also won rookie-of-the-year honors and the Michigan State Midget Championship. Ryan and his father started to think that Ryan might have a career in racing. When he was racing quarter midgets, it just seemed like a fun weekend activity for the whole family. Now, it was becoming clear that Ryan had real talent.

Ryan's success continued in the 1994 Midget racing season. In 1995, he entered the United States Auto Club (USAC) Midget Series, another step on the path to the NASCAR Cup series. Ryan ran into a few problems that year, getting into several accidents. However, he won the USAC Midget Rookie of the Year award, and he placed tenth in the standings.

College

All throughout high school, Ryan had carefully balanced racing with his studies. This rigorous schedule didn't leave him a lot of time for dating or partying, but that was fine with Ryan. His most important goal was to make it in racing. In 1996, he graduated from LaSalle High School in South Bend, Indiana. Ryan graduated in the top 20 of his class and was a member of the National Honor Society.

In the fall of 1996, Ryan began classes at Purdue University in West Lafayette, Indiana. Purdue was close enough to home that Ryan could stay with his family on the weekends and work on his race car. Purdue also had a great engineering program, which is what he planned to study.

Once again, Ryan did not have a lot of extra time for fun at Purdue. Sometimes, it was a struggle to succeed at both college and racing. He told Indianapolis Monthly in 2002, "There were times when I wanted to quit school.

It was a lot of hard work on both fronts, but I'm glad I hung in there." He knew that getting a degree was important to his parents. He also knew it would be good to have an education in case his racing career ever ended.

An engineering degree would also be helpful to his racing career. Ryan decided that to get the most out of his engineering program, he should take many different types of engineering classes. His college adviser helped him design a special degree in vehicle structural engineering. It combined several engineering programs into one. Ryan also took communications courses, including public speaking. He hoped all of his classes would come in handy if he became a NASCAR star.

CHAPTER 2

Becoming a Professional Racer

While Newman was still at Purdue, he continued racing on the weekends. He worked his way up through the ranks in various divisions in the United States Automobile Club (USAC) Midget Series. He won rookie-of-the-year honors in the 1996 Silver Crown Series and was the 1999 USAC Silver Crown Champion.

Looking for the Right Team

Newman knew that to advance his career, he would need to join a racing team. Racing is an expensive sport. For instance, engines alone can cost as much as $40,000 each, and some drivers use up to six cars each racing season. A driver can go through 40 tires—each costing $400—in just one race.

Being part of a team is the best way to afford the costs. The owner

It is important that the pit crew works fast. However, they need to be very precise. One small mistake can mean the difference between a smooth race and an accident.

is the head of the team. He or she owns the cars and pays the drivers and crew members. Some teams provide a salary to drivers. Other teams pay drivers part of their race winnings. To cover expenses, the owner gets money from a few sources. One is from prize money from winning races. Another source is sponsors. Companies will pay a team owner to put their logo on the car and the driver's jacket or helmet.

During the 1998 and 1999 seasons, Newman tried out for a few different racing teams. However, none of them seemed quite right. Newman knew that he wanted to make a big splash when he entered the NASCAR series, so he wanted to wait for just the right team. He also had to finish college.

One team that he was impressed with was Penske Racing. Owned by Roger Penske, a former NASCAR driver, the team was very successful. Penske had a good eye for picking talented drivers, and his team won many races. Don Miller, a co-owner of Penske Racing, met with Newman and his father in February 2000 at Daytona. Miller was equally impressed with Newman, and he decided to give the young racer a test drive.

Tryout in St. Louis

They agreed to hold the test in March during Newman's spring break. They chose the Gateway International Raceway in St. Louis, Missouri. The Penske team sent a car for Newman to drive. Penske also sent Buddy Baker, a former NASCAR racer, as their scout.

Newman drove slowly and cautiously at first. He didn't want to crash a car that didn't belong to him. However, when Baker gave his approval for Newman to speed up, he took off. Baker was very impressed and called Don Miller at Penske. He told Miller to sign Newman to the team as quickly as possible. Even

Newman (shown here with Roger Penske) is sponsored by Alltel, a communications company. In return for sponsorship, Alltel's logo is displayed on Newman's cars and racing gear.

Newman was happy with his performance. After a few more tests at other tracks that spring, Penske asked Newman to join the team.

A Successful First Year in NASCAR

In the spring of 2000, Newman moved to North Carolina. He bought a house on Lake Norman, near the Penske headquarters in Mooresville, North Carolina. Newman had to finish three credits to get his degree from Purdue. He decided to do that from North Carolina

Teamwork is extremely important in racing. Newman depends on Matt Borland, his crew chief *(right)*, to keep his cars running at top speed.

by taking an online course. In the meantime, he began preparing for his first season with Penske by working on his car with his team. Matt Borland, a mechanical engineer, would be Newman's crew chief.

In June 2000, Newman began competing in the Automobile Racing Club of America (ARCA) Series, a division of NASCAR. His first race was at the Michigan International Speedway. Despite some engine problems, he finished in the top ten. Newman won his second race, and then his third. He won his fourth race, too. Not only did he win the fourth race, he also broke the track speed record by going 186.780 miles per hour (300.593 kilometers per hour).

A WEEK OF RACING

During the racing season, the driver and pit crew have little time off. The race week usually begins on Tuesday at 7AM, when the crew starts their preparations. They do drills to practice their pit routines, and they all work out regularly.

By the middle of the week, the crew is busy preparing the car for that weekend's race. Once the car is ready, a truck will transport it to the track. The driver and crew usually drive or fly to the racetrack on Thursday night. The crew unloads the car on Friday and presents it to NASCAR officials for inspection.

After the car has been inspected, the driver does a practice run on the track. Based on the driver's feedback, the team makes adjustments to the car. The race for pole position usually takes place on Friday. On Saturday, the driver does another practice run, and the team makes more adjustments to the car. Sunday is the long race day. The driver and the crew review the race on Monday and get a rare chance to rest—but not for long. Tuesday, they begin all over again.

Near the end of his first season, Newman went to Phoenix to try a NASCAR Cup race. Although he qualified for the race, he had lots of trouble with his car. He finished the race 41st out of 43 cars. Although they were disappointed, Newman and the team looked at it as a learning experience.

The ABC Plan

During the off-season, Newman and the rest of the Penske team began planning for 2001. They decided that the way to give Newman the most driving experience was to do many races on various racetracks. He raced in three series: the Automobile Racing Club of America (ARCA), NASCAR's Busch Series, and NASCAR's Winston Cup Series (now Nextel Cup). Each series has its own rules and regulations. Usually, a driver races in only one series.

Penske Racing decided that Newman should enter races in all series. Penske thought of this as the "ABC" plan, with ABC standing for the initials of each of the three series. This plan would be hard for the racing crew. Because the rules for each series are different, they would have to have three types of cars ready at all times. The idea was to have Newman concentrate on just one race at a time, rather than focusing on winning any of the series. Penske wanted the new racer to get all of the experience that he could.

Roger Penske retired from racing in 1965 and started a racing team. He is also a successful businessman and owns car dealerships and rental trucks.

Getting into Trouble on the Track

Newman won his very first race of the 2001 season. It was an ARCA race at Daytona, Florida. The second race didn't go as well, and Newman had some on-track problems with other cars. During the race, he got between two other cars, bumping both of them. Other drivers involved in the incidents believed he caused some near-accidents, and they complained to race officials. In his fourth race, Newman got into a scrape with Tim Fedewa's car. In a later lap, Fedewa bumped Newman's car. Later, Newman slammed into Fedewa's car. After the race, officials put Newman and his team on probation. The team also had to pay a fine.

With this early-season trouble, Roger Penske considered cutting Newman from the team. However, Don Miller stuck up for Newman. He convinced Penske to let them try a Cup race in June in Michigan. Penske agreed but said Newman and his team would have to do well. If not, they would probably be dropped from Penske Racing.

Penske ended up attending the Michigan race in place of Miller, who was in the hospital. The team owner talked with his driver through a headset all through the race, and Newman ended up finishing fifth. Penske left the race convinced that Newman had the talent to stay on the team. He would just have to find a way to stay out of trouble.

Newman's troubles weren't over yet. At a Busch race in Chicago, he ran into another car with only a few laps to go. His car was damaged, and his front left tire was flat. His brakes were also damaged and were no longer working properly. Ignoring the black flag the official used to signal him to get off the track, Newman continued driving. Unhappy that Newman ignored the flag, NASCAR officials fined him and decided to keep him on probation.

Turning Things Around

Newman took part of July off to prepare for upcoming races. When he returned to the track, he won a Busch Series race in Michigan, staying in front of the pack for most of the race. Besides his win at Michigan, Newman had another thing to be proud of that summer. He completed the remaining three credits for Purdue. In August, he received his degree in structural engineering.

Newman is very gracious with fans and often takes time to sign autographs. He especially enjoys meeting his young fans.

Although the 2001 season was full of ups and downs, Newman and his crew learned a lot and worked well together. That year, Newman improved dramatically as a driver. He finished the season with two wins, five top-five finishes, and 11 top-ten finishes. Newman also began to enjoy that he was becoming a star. People asked him to sign their Ryan Newman hats and T-shirts. He was happy to see fans who were so excited to meet him and get his autograph. As he told *Indianapolis Monthly* in 2002, "NASCAR is where it's at, and I'm just thankful to be a part of it."

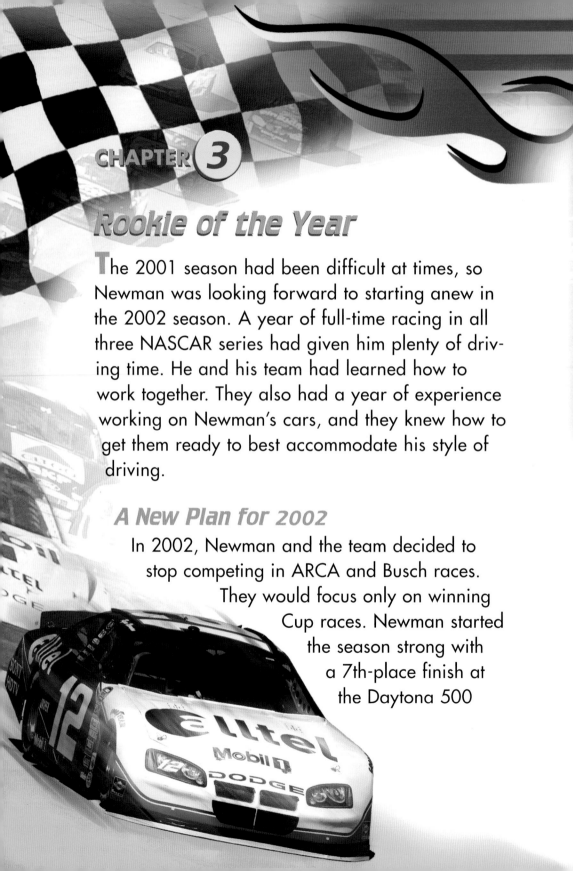

CHAPTER 3

Rookie of the Year

The 2001 season had been difficult at times, so Newman was looking forward to starting anew in the 2002 season. A year of full-time racing in all three NASCAR series had given him plenty of driving time. He and his team had learned how to work together. They also had a year of experience working on Newman's cars, and they knew how to get them ready to best accommodate his style of driving.

A New Plan for 2002

In 2002, Newman and the team decided to stop competing in ARCA and Busch races. They would focus only on winning Cup races. Newman started the season strong with a 7th-place finish at the Daytona 500

Newman leads the pack at the start of the New Hampshire 300 on September 15, 2002. During races, Newman keeps in constant contact with Borland by radio.

in February. In his next race he finished 14th, and in the following three races, he finished in the top ten.

Newman's early successes were followed by four terrible starts. He turned things around with a second-place finish, and went on to claim a thrilling win in the Winston in Concord, North Carolina, in May. From then on, Newman was on a roll. In the next 25 races, he finished in the top ten 17 times.

Newman's First Win and a Rookie Award

In September, Newman won his first Cup race, the New Hampshire 300. Although he had won the Winston earlier in the year, it didn't count toward his series points. So, New Hampshire counted as his first official win in the Cup series. Although the race was shortened due to rain, Newman led the pack for more than half of the 207 laps.

In addition to his first win, Newman was attracting attention for another reason. On the Friday before a race, drivers compete in time trials to see who will be first to start that Sunday's race. Newman won the qualifying race six times in the 2002 season. That meant he started Sunday's race in first place—also known as the pole position. This was a record for a rookie Cup driver. It earned Newman one of his nicknames: Mr. Friday.

Newman finished the 2002 season ranked sixth overall in the field of 87 Cup drivers. Even more exciting, he narrowly beat Jimmie Johnson for the Raybestos Rookie of the Year award. Would Newman be able to repeat his amazing success in his second season?

A Rocky Start to a New Season

Newman's 2003 season did not get off to a good start. In the early part of the opening race, the Daytona 500, he was involved in a very serious crash. On lap 56, his car was hit by another driver. The right back wheel came

This crash ended Newman's chances to finish the Daytona 500 on February 16, 2003. Although the car came apart, the protective compartment and safety features saved Newman's life.

off, causing the car to spin out. Skidding off the track and through the grass, his car rolled over and over again. To the horror of Newman's crew, his family, and race spectators, the car began to come apart. Finally, the mangled auto came to rest upside down.

Newman was sore from the crash but was otherwise unhurt. Regulation NASCAR cars have many safety features that protect a driver in the event of a crash. After

NEWMAN'S PIT CREW

Newman often said he couldn't win without his pit crew and crew chief, Matt Borland. Both engineers, Borland and Newman are able to communicate about the car and any problems. The two men get along well and are able to remain calm in high-pressure racing situations.

Newman's pit crew is extremely efficient and can complete a pit stop in 12 to 14 seconds. They train constantly to improve their time, often videotaping pit stops to learn from their performance in the previous races.

Seven crew members enter the pit during a pit stop. The jack man raises the car so tires can be changed. Two tire changers remove and put on new tires. Two tire carriers haul the 80-pound (36 kilograms) tires, and two crew members fill the car with fuel.

the death of Dale Earnhardt in a crash at Daytona in 2001, NASCAR added many safety requirements. In addition to helmets with full face shields, drivers also wear neck collars. Their protective suits are made of fire-retardant material. The front and back of each car is designed to collapse on impact. The front of the car pushes the engine down in crashes, instead of back toward the driver. Gas tanks are surrounded by foam so they won't explode. The compartment where the driver sits is filled with padding and protective bars, and the driver is held in place by a harness.

The crash upset Newman. When he had first started to slide through the grass, he was already thinking ahead to whether the crew would be able to get the car in shape so he could re-enter the race. By the time the car came to a rest, however, it was clear that there was no way he could go on. February and March brought additional setbacks. Newman struggled with car trouble, as well as getting in another crash. In April, he crashed once again at the Talladega Superspeedway. The one upside was that he managed to score a win at Texas at the end of March.

Wins and Accusations

A race at Dover International Speedway in June brought Newman another hard-won victory. Near the end of the race, Newman's car lost power steering. He had to use every ounce of strength to steer it through the turns in the last few laps.

In June, Newman ran into more car trouble. In a race in Michigan, his car caught on fire. He thought the fire would go out, but it quickly spread to the driver compartment. Newman managed to pull over and use his fire extinguisher to put out the fire. Luckily, his helmet and suit

Despite setbacks, such as this car fire at Michigan International Speedway in June 2003, that season was Newman's most successful to date. Other drivers praise Newman's bravery, toughness, and concentration.

protected most of his body, and he only sustained burns on his chin.

Things improved from there. Newman claimed two wins in July, one in August, two in September, and one in October. These victories caused some people to accuse the young driver of cheating. They just couldn't believe the good gas mileage he was getting, and they thought he must be breaking the rules. However, NASCAR conducts extremely careful inspections of cars before and after every race. It found nothing wrong with Newman's cars or gas tanks.

Newman's eight wins in 2003 were a huge accomplishment, especially for a driver only in his second season. However, he didn't win the Cup. He came in sixth in the standings, partly because he did not finish seven races. NASCAR assigns a certain number of points for wins for each race. Drivers can also get points for other things, like leading a lap during the race. At the end of the season, the points are tallied and the person with the highest total wins the Cup.

After the 2003 season, NASCAR changed the scoring rules. Now, after the 26th race of the season, the top ten drivers get to compete in the Chase for the Championship. Any other drivers that are 400 points or less from the points leader can compete in the Chase as well. At the beginning of the Chase, NASCAR adjusts the points for the drivers. The top driver gets 5,050 points, the second-place driver gets 5,045, the third-place driver gets 5,040, and so on.

Although he didn't win the Cup, Newman did win other awards for his 2003 season. He was named SPEED Channel Driver of the Year, NMPA Richard Petty Driver of the Year, Benny Kahn/*Daytona Beach News Journal* Driver of the Year, and the *Sporting News'* Dale Earnhardt Toughest Driver of the Year. Earnhardt was one of Newman's heroes, and winning the award meant a lot to him. He was given the award in recognition of his fearless driving style, as well as the extensive prep work he does with his team before each race.

In 2005, Newman drove in several Busch Series races. In the Busch Series races, Newman drives the #39 Dodge, rather than the #12 Dodge he uses in Nextel Cup races.

After winning all of those awards, Newman still had one more reason to celebrate. On January 3, 2004, he married Krissie Boyle, whom he had met on a blind date in the fall of 2001. Boyle has a degree in criminal justice from Shippensburg University in Pennsylvania. She didn't know anything about racing when she first met Newman, but she quickly learned.

Leaving His Mark

Newman had fewer wins in 2004. He suffered a number of crashes during the season, and in some races his cars had engine trouble. Although he won the pole position nine times, he had just two wins. One was in Michigan in June; the other was in Dover, Delaware, in September. This left Newman in seventh place in the Cup standings. Although he didn't win the Cup, he told the *Sporting News* that he was happy to just have been successful. He told them, "No matter what you're doing, as long as you leave your mark, that's what's important."

Newman continued to leave his mark in 2005. Once again he led NASCAR with eight pole positions. He won the Bud Pole Award for the fourth year in a row. He won one Cup race in September and placed sixth in Cup standings. In addition to his Cup races, Newman competed in some Busch Series races. At one point, he won five Busch races in a row, winning a total of six for the whole season. Racing in the Busch Series provided Newman with extra time behind the wheel, which he hoped would pay off in the 2006 season.

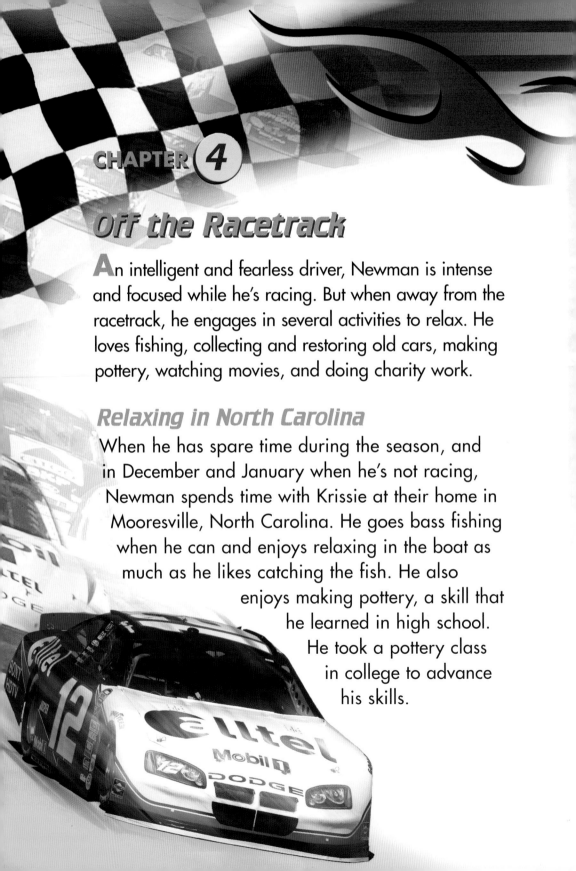

CHAPTER 4

Off the Racetrack

An intelligent and fearless driver, Newman is intense and focused while he's racing. But when away from the racetrack, he engages in several activities to relax. He loves fishing, collecting and restoring old cars, making pottery, watching movies, and doing charity work.

Relaxing in North Carolina

When he has spare time during the season, and in December and January when he's not racing, Newman spends time with Krissie at their home in Mooresville, North Carolina. He goes bass fishing when he can and enjoys relaxing in the boat as much as he likes catching the fish. He also enjoys making pottery, a skill that he learned in high school. He took a pottery class in college to advance his skills.

Newman shows off his winning time at the trial for the Winston Cup Coca-Cola 600 on May 23, 2003. Newman's car hit 185.312 miles an hour (298.231 kilometers per hour) in one lap.

Collecting Cars

Newman has quite a collection of cars. Included are the ones he drove in quarter midget and midget races. His father kept two of these cars in his garage. Newman was able to track down another on eBay.

Ryan and Krissie Newman, pictured here with their dog Mopar, announced their book, *Pit Road Pets*, at the Daytona Beach International Speedway in Daytona Beach, Florida on February 10, 2006.

The rest of Newman's car collection consists of classic cars. He has a 1928 Ford Roadster, a 1939 Hudson Sedan, and several models from the 1950s. One of them is a 1953 Plymouth Cranbrook given to him by Don Miller. The Plymouth is the same model as the car Newman drove when he was in high school and college. Miller gave it to him after he won his first Cup race. Newman also still has his grandfather's 1974 Triumph TR-6.

Charity Work

Newman and his wife are interested in using their time and money to help others. In January 2005, they started the Ryan Newman Foundation. Their organization was set up to help animals, save wildlife and the environment, and give scholarships to race car drivers who want to go to college. The foundation has donated $400,000 to a local animal shelter and $19,000 to help victims of Hurricane Katrina who had lost their pets.

Through the Ryan Newman Foundation, Krissie and Ryan have published a book titled *Pit Road Pets*. All of the money the foundation makes from the book will be donated to the Humane Society of Catawba County, North Carolina.

Looking Ahead

In 2006, Newman got a new teammate at Penske Racing: Kurt Busch. Newman had a sometimes difficult relationship with a former teammate, racing legend Rusty Wallace. His team and Wallace's team were sometimes at odds and did not always share helpful racing information. Newman hopes things will be different with Busch, and he's looking forward to learning from his new teammate.

In 2007, NASCAR will introduce a new car design called the Car of Tomorrow. All drivers will be required to drive the Car of Tomorrow, which will be easier to handle than current stock cars, and will also have more safety features. Until it is introduced, however, Newman

Newman is pictured here after winning the NASCAR Busch Series Food City 250 on August 26, 2005, in Bristol, Tennessee. Newman is known to his racing friends as Rocketman.

and his team will continue to try to improve the Dodges he drives.

Newman is extremely proud of what he and his team have accomplished. He has always tried to do his best and always works hard. He is honored to have won so many races so early in his career, but winning just makes him push himself even harder.

Awards

1985 Quarter Midget National Champion

1988 Quarter Midget National Champion;
      Quarter Midget Hall of Fame

1993 All American Midget Series Champion
        and Rookie of the Year
      Michigan State Midget Champion

1995 USAC Midget Series Rookie of the Year

1996 USAC Silver Crown Series Rookie of
        the Year

1999 USAC Coors Light Silver Bullet Series
        National Champion

2002 Raybestos Rookie of the Year
      Bud Pole Award

2003 SPEED Channel Driver of the Year
      NMPA Richard Petty Driver of the Year
      Benny Kahn/*Daytona Beach News
        Journal* Driver of the Year
      Sporting News' Dale Earnhardt Toughest
        Driver of the Year
      Bud Pole Award

2004 Bud Pole Award

2005 Bud Pole Award

Glossary

asphalt A substance used for paving roads.

efficient Producing good results quickly.

fine Money paid as punishment.

mechanical engineer Someone who studies how tools and machines work.

open-wheel race car A car that has wheels that stick out past the body of the car.

probation A period of time when a driver is closely watched for any bad behavior.

qualify To meet the requirements that allow a driver to enter a race.

regulation A rule that determines how something should be done.

rookie A beginner; a first-year player in a sport.

scout Someone who attends a sporting event to search for new talent.

slot car A toy race car that can be raced on a grooved track.

spectator Someone who watches a performance or race.

stock car A racing car that is similar to everyday street cars.

street car A car that is driven on a regular road instead of a racetrack.

structural engineer Someone who studies structures such as walls, bridges, and buildings.

For More Information

NASCAR
P.O. Box 2875
Daytona Beach, FL 32120
(386) 253-0611
Web site: http://www.nascar.com

The Official Ryan Newman Fan Club
P.O. Box 3718
South Bend, IN 46619-0718
Web site: http://www.ryan12newman.com

Penske Racing
136 Knob Hill Road
Mooresville, NC 28117
Web site: http://www.penskeracing.com

Ryan Newman Foundation, Inc.
P.O. Box 5998
Statesville, NC 28687
Web site: http://www.ryannewmanfoundation.org

Web Sites

Due to the changing nature of Internet links, Rosen Publishing has developed an online list of Web sites related to the subject of this book. This site is updated regularly. Please use this link to access the list:

http://www.rosenlinks.com/bw/ryne

For Further Reading

Barber, Phil. *From Finish to Start: A Week in the Life of a NASCAR Racing Team*. Maple Plain, MN: Tradition Books, 2004.

Buckley, James, Jr. *NASCAR*. New York, NY: Dorling Kindersley Children, 2005.

Buckley, James, Jr. *Speedway Superstars*. Pleasantville, NY: Reader's Digest Children's Books, 2004.

Miller, Timothy, and Steve Milton. *NASCAR Now*. Buffalo, NY: Firefly Books, 2004.

Sports Illustrated. *Full Throttle: From Daytona to Darlington*. New York, NY: Sports Illustrated Books, 2004.

Woods, Bob. *Earning a Ride: How to Become a NASCAR Driver*. Chanhassen, MN: Child's World, 2003.

Bibliography

Barber, Phil. *From Finish to Start: A Week in the Life of a NASCAR Racing Team*. Maple Plain, MN: Tradition Books, 2004.

Buckley, James, Jr. *Speedway Superstars*. Pleasantville, NY: Reader's Digest Children's Books, 2004.

Cavin, Curt. "Big Time." *AutoWeek*, Vol. 51, Issue 5, January 29, 2001.

Cothren, Larry. "Stock Car Racing's Personalities & Biographies: Ryan Newman Interview." Stockcarracing.com. Retrieved March 1, 2006 (http://www.stockcarracing.com/thehistoryof/bio/134_0411_ ryan_newman_int/index.html).

MacGregor, Jeff. *Sunday Money: Speed! Lust! Madness! Death! A Hot Lap Around America with NASCAR*. New York, NY: HarperCollins, 2005.

Miller, Robin. "Flyin' Ryan." *Indianapolis Monthly*, Vol. 25, Issue 7, February 2002.

Miller, Timothy, and Steve Milton. *NASCAR Now*. Buffalo, NY: Firefly Books, 2004.

"Newman Wins Winston." *USA Today*, May 20, 2002, p. 9C.

Rodman, Dave. "Ten Questions with Ryan Newman." January 11, 2006. NASCAR.com. Retrieved February 15, 2006 (http:// www.nascar.com/2006/news/headlines/cup/01/11/ rnewman_10_questions/index.html).

Spencer, Lee. "Q&A Ryan Newman." *Sporting News*, Vol. 228, Issue 48, November 29, 2004.

Spencer, Lee. "2003 NASCAR Awards." *Sporting News*, Vol. 227, Issue 49, December 8, 2003.

Sports Illustrated. *Full Throttle: From Daytona to Darlington*. New York, NY: Sports Illustrated Books, 2004.

Williams, Deb. *Ryan Newman: Engineering Speed*. Champaign, IL: Sports Publishing LLC, 2004.

Index

About the Author

Simone Payment has a degree in psychology from Cornell University and a master's degree in elementary education from Wheelock College. She is the author of fifteen books for young adults. Her book *Inside Special Operations: Navy SEALs* (also from Rosen Publishing) won a 2004 Quick Picks for Reluctant Young Readers award from the American Library Association and is on the Nonfiction Honor List of Voice of Youth Advocates.

Photo Credits

Cover © Craig Jones/Getty Images; pp. 1, 27 © Donald Miralle/Getty Images; p. 5 © Chris Stanford/Getty Images; pp. 6–7, 37 © Jeff Gross/Getty Images; p. 11 © Tom Strickland/Associated Press, AP; p. 12 © Streeter Lecka/Getty Images; pp. 17, 25 © Jamie Squire/Getty Images; p. 19 © Darrell Ingham/Getty Images; p. 20 © Doug Pensinger/Getty Images; pp. 23, 34 © Robert Laberge/Allsport/Getty Images; p. 29 © Karl Ronstrom/Reuters/Corbis; p. 32 © Dave Frechette/Associated Press, AP; p. 38 © Paul Kizzle/Associated Press, AP; p. 40 © Rusty Jarrett.

Designer: Gene Mollica